Co

Wherever you see me, you'll find activities to try and questions to answer.

The Balmy Bahamas

The Caribbean Sea lies between Florida and South America. With beautiful beaches, warm seas, and sunny weather all year round, the Caribbean is a popular vacation destination. Each year, for example, up to five million people visit the Bahamas, the island group closest to the United States.

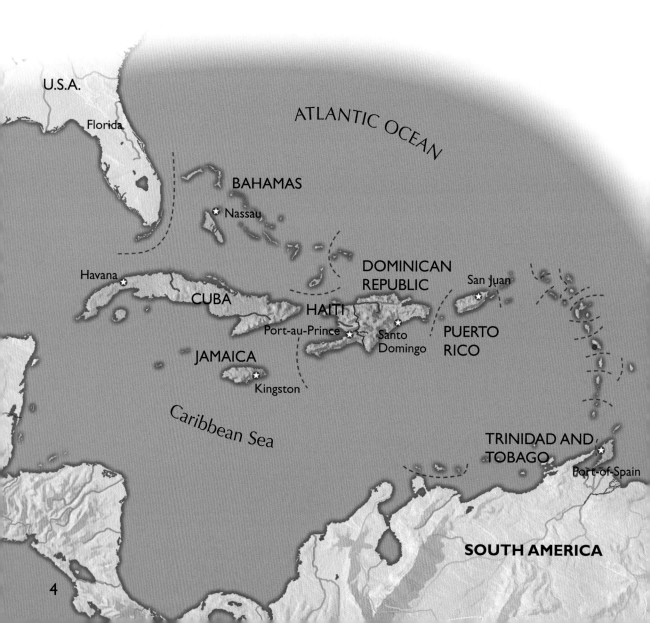

U.S.A.

Florida

ATLANTIC OCEAN

BAHAMAS

★ Nassau

DOMINICAN REPUBLIC

San Juan ★

Havana ★

CUBA

HAITI

Port-au-Prince ★

Santo Domingo ★

PUERTO RICO

JAMAICA

Kingston ★

Caribbean Sea

TRINIDAD AND TOBAGO ★

Port-of-Spain

SOUTH AMERICA

The Commonwealth of the Bahamas is an archipelago that includes 30 islands with people living on them, 661 uninhabited small coral islands called *cays*, and more than 2,000 exposed reefs. The total land area is 5,382 square miles. The area of reefs is estimated to be another 765 square miles.

Area of the Smallest U.S. States (Square Miles)

New Jersey	8,722
Connecticut	5,544
Delaware	1,954
Rhode Island	1,545

Compare the land area of the Bahamas and each of the states above. What is the total area of land and reefs in the Bahamas?

archipelago   a large body of water with many islands

Wonderful Weather

The weather is warm all year round in the Bahamas. January is the coolest month, with temperatures that range from an average minimum of 62°F to an average maximum of 77°F. The hottest month is August, with temperatures that are about 12 degrees higher than those in January. The average rainfall is 56 inches, with most of the rain falling between May and October.

Sunshine Statistics		
Month	Day Length (Hours)	Hours of Bright Sunshine
January	10.3	7.1
February	11.3	7.6
March	12.0	8.3
April	12.7	9.2
May	13.3	8.7
June	13.7	7.7
July	13.5	8.8
August	13.0	8.6
September	12.3	7.1
October	11.6	7.2
November	11.0	7.4
December	10.6	6.9

Calculate a) the average day length in the Bahamas, and b) the average number of hours of bright sunshine. Round your answers to the nearest tenth of an hour.

Make a Line Graph

To make a graph that shows the Sunshine Statistics on page 6, you will need a copy of the Blackline Master and a ruler.

1. Plot points to show the day length for each month.

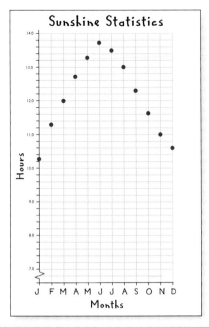

2. Draw lines to join the points. (Use a ruler.)

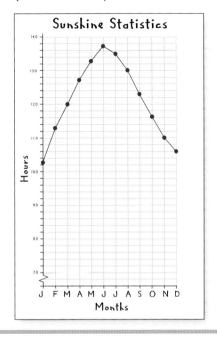

3. Use a different color to show the hours of bright sunshine.

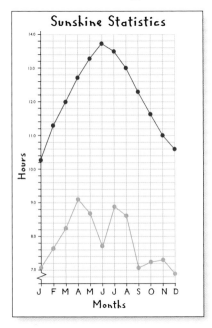

4. Label each line or create a color key for your graph.

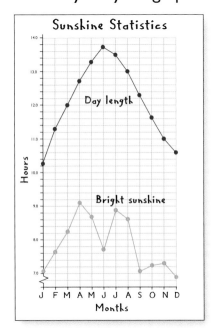

Sailing to the Bahamas

The Bahamas are within easy sailing distance of Florida. From Miami, for example, it is only 44 miles to Gun Cay, and the distance from West Palm Beach to the island of Grand Bahama is about 56 miles. Each year, more than 20,000 boats travel from Florida to the Bahamas. These vessels range in size from small yachts sailed by one person to huge cruise ships that carry more than 3,000 passengers.

Fees for Vessels Entering the Bahamas

- Vessels under 35 feet $150
- Vessels 35 feet or greater $300
- Dinghies/tenders over 18 feet $150

Fees cover the captain and 3 passengers and include a 3-month fishing license.

Calculate the fee that each of the groups below must pay to enter the Bahamas.

Additional Fees

- $15 per person for additional passengers above 6 years of age
- $150 to extend fishing license for an additional 12 months
- If the vessel remains in the Bahamas for more than one year, $500 per year for each of the next two years

The Donovan family

John and Sue and their children, ages 16, 13, 8, and 5 years, are sailing a 57-foot yacht. They plan to spend 6 months in the Bahamas and want to be able to fish during that time.

The Santiagos

Juan and Maria are retired. They plan to live in the Bahamas aboard their 32-foot catamaran for $2\frac{1}{2}$ years. They are not interested in fishing.

Tourism Statistics

The islands of the Bahamas are the most popular destination for Caribbean cruise ships. In the year 2004 alone, 3.7 million cruise passengers visited the Bahamas, and another 1.4 million tourists arrived by air. As the population of the Bahamas is only about 300,000, the tourists greatly outnumber the locals! Tourism provides employment for about half of the 156,000 people in the Bahamas' work force.

Cruise ships in the port of Nassau, capital of the Bahamas

Tourists Visiting the Bahamas*

Number of Tourists (millions) vs. Year

Number of Tourists* Visiting the Bahamas

Month	Number
January	95,948
February	119,347
March	165,185
April	125,112
May	126,863
June	135,493
July	137,050
August	128,586
September	70,193
October	86,900
November	102,699
December	109,518

Estimate and then calculate the total number of tourists for the year at the right. Then use the graph to figure out which year this data is for.

* Does not include cruise-ship passengers

11

Tourism Revenue

Tourism is the most important industry of the Bahamas. Each year, tourists contribute more than 1.5 billion dollars to the local economy. Figures from 1999 show that the average tourist stayed in the Bahamas for five days and spent about $200 each day. However, an average cruise-ship passenger spent only about $60 altogether in the Bahamas, as the cost of a cruise includes meals, entertainment, and so on.

How the Tourist Dollar Is Spent in the Bahamas
($200 Daily Total)

Legend:
- ☐ Accommodations
- ☐ Meals and Drinks
- ☐ Transportation
- ☐ Entertainment
- ☐ Shopping
- ☐ Other

Use the pie chart to estimate how much the average tourist spends each day on—
- entertainment.
- meals and drinks.

Use the pie chart to help you complete this sentence: The average tourist to the Bahamas spends about $58 per day on _____ .

Pinpointing Position

In an area such as the Bahamas, it is very important for sailors to know the exact location of their boat. In the past, this involved using an instrument called a *sextant* to measure the angle between the horizon and the Sun. The sailor would consult a detailed nautical almanac to determine the exact latitude and longitude and would then find that position on a map or chart.

Learning to use a sextant requires a considerable amount of training and practice. Today, some people still use a sextant, but many sailors find it easier and more accurate to use electronic navigation tools.

nautical almanac   a calendar that shows information about the daily position of bodies such as the Sun, Moon, and stars

Latitude

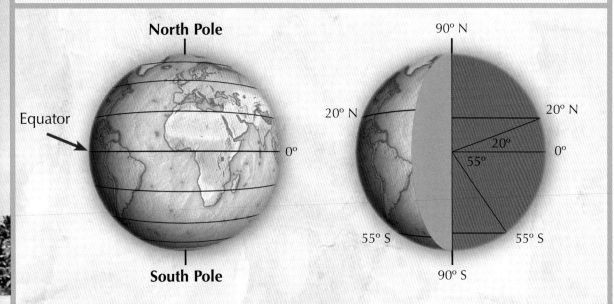

Lines of latitude are labeled in degrees north or south of the equator, which has a latitude of 0°. (Angles are measured from the center of Earth.)

Longitude

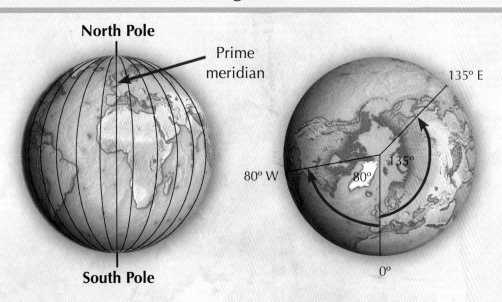

Lines of longitude are labeled in degrees east or west of the prime meridian, which runs through Greenwich, a town near London, England. The longitude of the prime meridian is 0°.

Location, Location

The islands of the Bahamas lie north of the equator and west of the prime meridian. They are between the latitudes of 20 and 27 degrees north and between the longitudes of 72 and 79 degrees west. Sailors used detailed navigation charts to pinpoint the location of the many islands and reefs of the Bahamas.

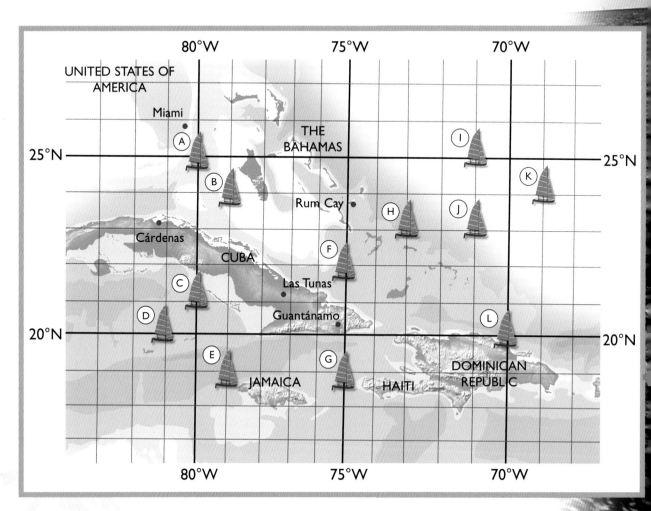

Figure It Out

1. Which of the yachts (A to K) is located at grid reference—

   a. 20°N 70°W? b. 25°N 71°W?

   c. 21°N 80°W? d. 24°N 69°W?

   e. 19°N 75°W? f. 23°N 73°W?

2. Write the grid reference for each of the other six yachts.

3. In which country is the grid reference point—

   a. 25°N 76°W? b. 26°N 81°W?

   c. 19°N 70°W? d. 21°N 76°W?

4. Which town in Cuba is closest to—

   a. 20°N 75°W? b. 23°N 81°W?

5. Give the reference for the grid-line intersection that is closest to—

   a. Miami, Florida.

   b. Las Tunas, Cuba.

   c. Rum Cay, Bahamas.

Today, the Global Positioning System takes a lot of the hard work out of navigation.
A GPS device uses simultaneous signals from four satellites to pinpoint its exact location.
Although GPS devices can give longitude and latitude readings, many people are starting to use a simpler grid system called *UTM,* or *Universal Transverse Mercator.*

Sounding the Depths

With so many reefs and areas of shallow water, it would be very easy for boats to run aground in the Bahamas. For many years, sailors have used paper charts that show the depth of the water and the location of reefs and other shipping hazards. These days, most vessels also carry a depth sounder—an electronic device that measures the depth of the water.

hazard　a danger or risk

A depth sounder measures the time it takes for a signal to travel from the bottom of a boat to the seabed and back again. Then it uses that measurement to calculate the depth of the water.

If a signal took 1.6 seconds to travel to the seabed and back, approximately how far did it travel? (Use the graph to find out.) How deep was the water?

Distance Traveled by Sound Through Water

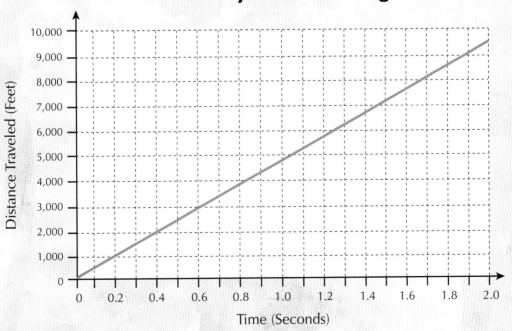

Into the Deep

The Bahamas are ideal for snorkeling and diving. The sea is warm and clear—the underwater visibility is about 100 feet, and the water temperature never drops below 72°F! In the Bahamas, scuba divers can explore coral reefs and sunken wrecks, swim with dolphins, or try to identify some of the many species of colorful fish.

Did You Know?

The word *scuba* comes from the initials of the words *Self-Contained Underwater Breathing Apparatus.*

Dive Packages (Typical Costs)

1 dive	$35
2 dives	$65
3 dives	$90
4 dives	$115
5 dives	$140
6 dives	$155
10 dives	$240

Compare the cost of a single dive with the average cost of each dive in—
- a 2-dive package.
- a 4-dive package.
- a 5-dive package.
- a 10-dive package.

Avoiding the Bends

As water gets deeper, water pressure increases. For scuba divers this means that, as they go deeper, more nitrogen is absorbed into their blood from the air they breathe. If a diver returns to the surface too quickly, this nitrogen can form bubbles in the bloodstream and body tissues, causing a decompression sickness nicknamed the *bends.* To help avoid getting the bends, scuba divers use tables that show how long they can stay at a certain depth.

The latest dive watches can show many measurements, including the current depth and how much longer the diver can safely remain at that depth.

decompression sickness   a condition that can cause pain in the muscles and joints, cramps, nausea, and paralysis

Scuba Diving Time Limits

Depth (Feet)	Time Limit (Minutes)
35	310
40	200
50	100
60	60
70	50
80	40
90	30
100	25
110	20
120	15
130	10
140	10
150	5

The table above shows the time limits for the first dive of a day. How long a diver can stay down on the next dive depends on the length and depth of the first dive.

Use data from the table to make this sentence true: On the first dive, a scuba diver can stay at a depth of ___ feet for ___ times as long as at a depth of ___ feet.

Sample Answers

Research Caribbean cruises. Make a graph to show some of the data you find. For example, you could compare the cost of staying in different cabins on a cruise ship.

Page 5   answers in square miles:
New Jersey: 3,340 bigger
Connecticut: 162 bigger
Delaware: 3,428 smaller
Rhode Island: 3,837 smaller
islands and reefs: 6,147

Page 6   a) 12.1 hours b) 7.9 hours

Page 9   Donovans: $465; Santiagos: $1,150

Page 11   1,402,894 tourists; 2002

Page 13   accommodations

Page 17   1. a. L   b. I   c. C   d. K   e. G   f. H

2. A 25°N 80°W   B 24°N 79°W
   D 20°N 81°W   E 19°N 79°W
   F 22°N 75°W   J 23°N 71°W

3. a. Bahamas   b. United States
   c. Dominican Rep.   d. Cuba

4. a. Guantánamo   b. Cárdenas

5. a. 26°N 80°W   b. 21°N 77°W   c. 24°N 75°W

Page 19   about 7,600 ft; about 3,800 ft

Page 21 $2.50; $6.25; $7.00; $11.00

Index